AIR,
the Invisible Ocean

by SIGMUND KALINA

Illustrations by Kazue Mizumura

AIR,
the Invisible Ocean

SCHOLASTIC BOOK SERVICES
NEW YORK · TORONTO · LONDON · AUCKLAND · SYDNEY · TOKYO

Thanks to my esteemed colleagues
William Devaux, Joseph Jeskie, and
John Manzella for their interest
and patience in the many conversations
that helped bring this book into being.

Text copyright © 1973 by Sigmund Kalina. Illustrations copyright © 1973 by Kazue Mizumura. This edition is published by Scholastic Book Services, a division of Scholastic Magazines, Inc., by arrangement with Lothrop, Lee & Shepard Company, a division of William Morrow & Company, Inc.

1st printing..September 1974

Printed in the U.S.A.

*For my infant grandson, Stefan.
In the years to come, may he inherit
a healthy environment.*

An ocean is exciting, with splashing waves and sandy beaches that disappear beneath the hidden rocks, anchored to the ocean floor. There, a community of animals hunt for food and find shelter in the sculptured, sandy bottom.

Like the creatures of the deep, you too live at the bottom of an ocean — an ocean which is deeper than any ocean of water. You spend your entire life at the bottom of an ocean of air!

This ocean of air reaches out in all directions — exploring the deepest mines, filling the emptiness above the highest mountains, and thinning out, far off into space. It surrounds our planet Earth, and is called the atmosphere.

You might think of the atmosphere as a blanket of air covering the earth, and stopping the sun's strong, burning rays from broiling all the plants and animals on our planet.

The atmosphere acts as a screen, allowing some of the sun's rays to slip through to the earth. At the same time, it blocks the earth's heat from quickly escaping into space. In this way, the earth and all its living things are kept warm and alive.

Without an atmosphere, our planet would have no burrowing earthworms, no chewing grasshoppers, no furry creatures darting about, no trees with nesting birds, and no seaweed-nibbling fish. Indeed, it would be a world without life!

Imagine the hot rays of the sun burning everything in sight, the nights so cold that everything would freeze. All this would happen if our planet Earth were not surrounded by an atmosphere of air.

This ocean of air is most unusual. You cannot see it, you cannot touch it, but you know it is there. You can feel it blowing against your cheek on a windy day.

The air is all around you — outside your home, inside your home, and inside you too.

It is not possible to cut out a block of air and store it on a shelf. It does not drip onto the floor, nor does air form puddles. Like smoke, air spreads out, filling any space it can reach. This kind of material is called a gas.

Through the ages, scientists tried to find out what air was made of.

Joseph Priestley, an English chemist who lived about two hundred years ago, wondered about the mystery of air. He watched things burn in it. He knew that animals and people use air to breathe. But Joseph Priestley did not know what was in the air that made all this happen.

One day, the English scientist placed a burning candle inside a large jar filled with air. He watched the candle flame burn bright and strong. Then he covered the jar. The flame began to flicker. It soon went out.

The scientist took a second jar filled with air. This time, he put a live mouse inside the jar. The mouse scurried around, trying to find a way out.

Then the scientist covered the jar. The mouse slowed down. In a short time it

died, just as the flaming candle had died out. Joseph Priestley quickly placed a fresh burning candle inside the jar with the dead mouse. The flame died down at once!

The English chemist stared at the jar, thinking about what he had seen. Reason told him that there was some gas in the air which had made the candle burn in the uncovered jar.

Whatever had caused the candle to burn must have been the same gas that

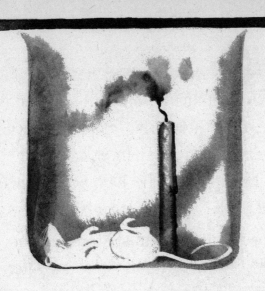

the mouse needed to breathe. In some way, the air which both the candle and the mouse used must have become "spoiled."

Would this happen someday to all the air in the world? How long would it be before all the air in the world spoiled, and everything died?

But in all the time up to Priestley's day, this had not happened. There must be some way, he thought, that nature keeps the air "unspoiled" all the time.

Joseph Priestley thought of all kinds of living things. He placed a small container filled with soil and a growing sprig of mint inside a jar in which the flame of a burning candle had just died out. He kept the jar covered about ten days.

The scientist then placed a fresh candle inside the jar. The lighted candle burned with a strong bright flame!

Priestley became excited. This time, he placed a live mouse and a sprig of mint inside another airtight jar. The

mouse continued to live. But when he removed the green mint plant, the mouse soon died.

Joseph Priestley had discovered nature's secret. The green plants make the difference. Somehow, they keep the air fresh . . . so things can burn in it, and living things can breathe it. The puzzled chemist did not understand how green plants do this.

Today, we know the answer to Joseph Priestley's puzzle. Air contains a colorless gas called oxygen, which makes things burn. Without oxygen, Priestley's candle could not have burned. The charcoal in your barbecue will not burn, the oil in the lamp will not give light, unless oxygen is present to make it burn with a bright flame.

Scientists have discovered another kind of "burning" — a slow burning without a flame. When people and animals breathe, they use the oxygen from the air to "burn" the food inside their cells. This gives them energy to grow, to move, and enough heat to warm their bodies.

Each cell of the body might be considered a tiny chemical factory in which energy is produced by burning. Scientists call this kind of burning inside cells "respiration."

Do not confuse respiration with "breathing." Breathing is filling your lungs with oxygen-filled air and blowing it out again. Respiration is more than breathing. Respiration is using oxygen inside your cells to give you energy.

Without respiration there is no energy; and without energy there is no life.

When most people think about breathing, they think of lungs or gills. An earthworm has no lungs or gills, but that does not stop it from breathing. The earthworm breathes through its thin skin, which is always kept moist. A slimy liquid oozes out through tiny openings in the skin. Oxygen from the air dissolves in this thin, watery film. In this way, the oxygen is held close to the skin, until it seeps through into the worm's body.

If the worm's skin should suddenly dry, the animal would die. That is why

an earthworm makes its home inside the damp earth. The burrows it digs funnel the air downward into the soil. When it rains hard, water fills these tunnels. This forces the worm to come out into the open to breathe.

All living things must have oxygen to stay alive.

Nature makes certain that all animals get their share of the life-giving air — not even forgetting the helpless unborn chick trapped inside its close-fitting shell.

Eggshells are carefully designed with many tiny pores through which the out-side air enters. Once inside the shell, the air gives up its precious oxygen to a network of hair-thin blood vessels pressed hard against the inside wall of the shell. Through this route, oxygen reaches the developing chick.

With the use of special instruments, scientists can find out how much oxygen is in the air. They tell us about one-fifth of the atmosphere is oxygen. The wonder of it is, that no matter how many things burn in it, or how many people and animals breathe it, the amount of oxygen in the air stays almost the same!

When breathing or burning occurs, oxygen is taken from the air and another gas, carbon dioxide, is released into the atmosphere. We know now that carbon dioxide was the gas that "spoiled" the air when Joseph Priestley's candle burned in the jar. It was the same gas that made the mouse die.

Now it is understood how the green mint plant kept the mouse alive inside the jar filled with carbon dioxide gas.

A green plant is always busy manufacturing food for itself and any number of animals that feed upon it. To do this, the plant keeps using the carbon dioxide from the air. In exchange, the green plant gives off oxygen, sending it back into the atmosphere. This helps keep a steady supply of oxygen for all living things to share.

In nature, there is no waste. Everything is used over and over again. Like oxygen, carbon dioxide gas finds its way back into the air.

When fallen leaves, broken twigs with berries, dried-up seeds that never had a chance to grow, and the dead plants, half buried in the earth, begin to decay, carbon dioxide they had used in growing is released again into the air. Once again, nature provides a balance.

Although carbon dioxide is heavier than air, it mixes into the atmosphere and is carried aloft with the restless air currents.

As our planet Earth spins in space, the atmosphere clings to it like a huge shell. Of the mixture of gases that is the atmosphere, more than three fourths is a gas called nitrogen.

Nitrogen is a sluggish gas. It does not combine freely with its companion gases in the atmosphere.

As the air moves its mixed cargo of gases over the land, puffs of wind dip down, bubbling the ocean top into a foamy mixture of atmospheric gases and sea water.

Both oxygen and carbon dioxide gases are caught up in the rippled surface waters, and then sink with them in the plunging currents.

The oxygen soon escapes back into the atmosphere, while most of the carbon dioxide remains mixed with the water. However, nitrogen is stubborn. It does not combine with water very readily. That is why the bulk of the atmosphere is nitrogen.

If nitrogen were to join easily with water, living things in oceans, lakes, and rivers would find it hard to survive.

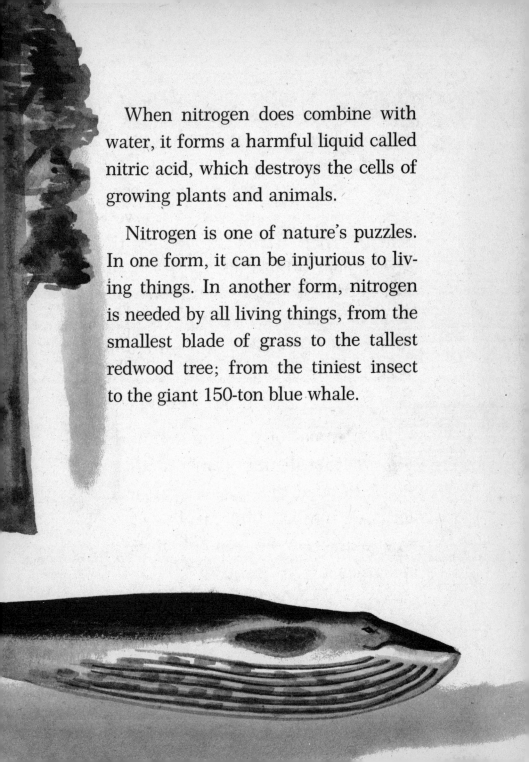

When nitrogen does combine with water, it forms a harmful liquid called nitric acid, which destroys the cells of growing plants and animals.

Nitrogen is one of nature's puzzles. In one form, it can be injurious to living things. In another form, nitrogen is needed by all living things, from the smallest blade of grass to the tallest redwood tree; from the tiniest insect to the giant 150-ton blue whale.

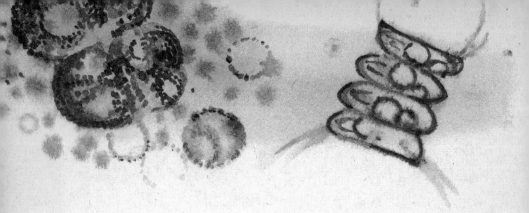

To supply this needed material, nature calls upon the green plants to capture some of the nitrogen as it reaches down to the earth's visible crust — a forest floor, a mountainside, or rolling hills and valleys.

Here armies of nitrogen-feeding bacteria wait for the nitrogen-filled air as it filters through the loosened earth. Bacteria are the tiniest of plants. One cell in size, they can be seen only through a microscope.

Many of these nitrogen-hungry bacteria live in the soil. Others live inside grape-like swellings bunched around the buried roots of alfalfa, clover, and bean plants.

These helpful bacteria take the nitrogen from air trapped in the soil, and use the nitrogen as food. As the nitrogen is taken into the bodies of the bacteria, it changes into a new form of nitrogen. When this is returned to the soil, it mixes readily with the soil water.

The ever-thirsty plant roots suck in the water, carrying nitrogen salts, sending it upward to the leaves. There, together with carbon dioxide, it is used by the plant's green cells to manufacture food and materials which help grow more leaves, longer and thicker stems, and deeper-spreading roots.

The variety of food produced by green plants is pleasing to the animal world — juicy berries for birds, meaty nuts for

squirrels, munchy leaves for deer, and all the sweet fruits you enjoy.

When living things die — a fallen bird, a broken branch, or a crushed earthworm — bacteria of decay make these things rot. This breaking down frees the nitrogen and returns it to the soil, to be used again by other plants. In this way, there is a steady supply of nitrogen, which green plants need to grow strong and healthy.

You could consider our atmosphere to be a far-reaching playground where gases and swarms of dust go back and forth between the sky and earth. The atmosphere takes up so much space, the dust particles go unnoticed, though they would add up to many tons! These bits of matter come from the surface of the earth, and out of the oceans, and some arrive from outer space.

Each time a plant or animal dies, its body crumbles into dust. Spiraled high on gusting winds, the dust mixes with drifts of loosened soil, floating pollen grains, and blowing seeds.

Rock dust and lava ash spouting from volcanoes, black soot of unburned bits of carbon fuming from smoking chimneys, and particles from windswept forest fires all add to this mixture.

The collection of smoke and dust in the air often interferes with the sun's rays on their way to Earth. The familiar colors that tint the sky — cool blues, warm pinks, cheerful yellows, and fiery reds — are caused by countless millions of minute specks of dust. Indeed, an atmosphere without dust would make our world look much different.

The oceans send their share of dust into the atmosphere. Waves splashing against rocky shores, together with the spray of wind-churned waters, free ever so many bits of salt grains. These are carried into the air inside millions of ballooning water droplets.

When storm clouds gather, you know from experience that they contain water. You know there is water in the air when it comes pouring down as rain, or when delicate snowflakes sprinkle the land in winter white.

How does water get into the atmosphere? Where does it come from?

About three fourths of the earth's surface is covered with the waters of oceans, lakes, and rivers. As the sun's rays sweep over these waters, their top layers become heated, which makes them very light. This changes the water into a gas that disappears into the air.

This process is called evaporation. The water in the atmosphere is known as water vapor — it has changed from a liquid to a dry gas. However, it still is water!

Very often, after a hard rain, you can see puddles on the ground. When the sun shines again, the puddles are soon gone. Evaporation made the water disappear back into the atmosphere.

Plants add their share of water to the air. They soak water up through their roots. The water they do not use seeps

out through tiny openings in the leaves
and then evaporates into the air.

Water escapes into the atmosphere
whenever animals and humans breathe.

Try this —
cup your hands in front of your mouth
and blow into them. You will feel the
warm wetness of your breath.

If you breathe onto a mirror held close
to your mouth, the mirror becomes cloudy
with tiny droplets of water. The warm
moisture in your breath cools against the
mirror; water vapor changes back into
liquid water. This is called condensation.

You can see condensation taking place
on a summer morning when the warm
moisture in the air touches the cooler
earth. Blades of grass sparkle with tiniest
water droplets. The grass is wet with dew.
And in the spring and fall, when the earth
is much colder, condensation produces a
thin, icy film of frost upon the ground.

Scientists have learned that when air rises high above the earth, it becomes cooled. In this cooler part of the atmosphere, particles of salt and dust attract water vapor. As the water vapor touches these specks, it changes into the tiniest droplets of liquid water. Droplets by the billions, sticking close together, form a cloud.

Some weather scientists believe that larger cloud droplets bump into smaller

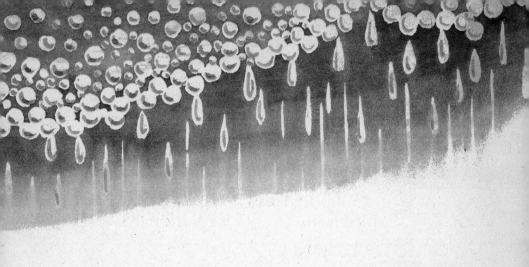

ones. When this happens, the droplets become much larger and heavier. The oversized droplets then fall as rain.

Almost two million square miles of the earth's surface is wrapped in the huge clinging veil of our atmosphere. With so much air in the world, it is amazing how light air actually is. It would take 800 milk containers filled with air to equal the weight of *one* milk container filled with water!

As you gaze up at the sky, you are looking through layers of air. Each layer presses down upon the layer under it, and all this air pushes down on the earth and everything upon it.

When air presses against the land, the ocean, or any other surface, it is called air pressure. Because there is so much of it, the air you carry on your shoulders weighs about one thousand pounds!

Under this great pressure of air, it would seem as though you might be crushed. However, air is also filling the many spaces inside your body. This inside pressure is just as strong as the outside pressure. Because of this, you do not feel the outer air pressing against you.

When you go up in an elevator or climb a high mountain, the air pressure outside your body becomes less, but the pressure inside you does not change. It keeps pushing outward. You start to feel uncomfortable. If you open your mouth, some of the air will rush out . . . now both inside and outside air pressures are the same. You begin to feel better again.

Did you know that air pushes against objects in all directions — sideways, down, and up? Have you ever gone to the circus, and watched the many-colored balloons flying in the air?

Those balloons are filled with helium, a gas which is much lighter than air. When a helium-filled balloon is set free, the air under the balloon pushes upward against the balloon — and up it goes!

Imagine we are going to take a journey high into the atmosphere. Our weather balloon is filled with helium. Hanging from the balloon is our sight-seeing cabin, strongly built to keep the inside air pressure from increasing, and bursting the cabin walls when it soars high into the atmosphere.

The sky is blue and clear, a sign of good weather. We begin to rise. The air around us is still warm from hugging the sun-heated earth. We drift higher. A stream of air shoots skyward, sucking in surrounding cooler, heavier air.

Suddenly, strong winds from the south begin to bump our cabin. Off to the west, the horizon is darkening with bands of grayish clouds, giving the sky a raggedy appearance.

The clouds become darker. Our instruments tell us the outside air pressure is falling. The winds begin to change. They blow toward the west . . . stronger and stronger they grow. A storm is on its way!

The western sky blackens. Sudden dark swirling clouds boil upward into huge mountains with flattened tops. Our cabin bumps and shakes violently in the strong angry winds. One minute, we are lifted high — then we plunge downward. Up and down we go, like a horse on a merry-go-round.

Suddenly, everything is blocked off. We are inside a dark thunderhead cloud. Crackling lightning zigzags through. Thunder crashes! Rain and icy pellets of hail rattle against the cabin walls, coming at us from all sides. There is nothing to do but wait!

We finally pass through the storm. The outside air pressure begins to rise. The temperature drops, and the winds become steady. Once again, the sky shows peacefully blue in all directions. In the distance, piled-up fluffy clouds with flattened bottoms, rounded sides, and dome-shaped tops seem to build white castles in the air.

The higher we go, the colder the air becomes, and the thinner is the atmosphere. Our instruments show us we have reached the height of three and one half miles — higher than Mount Whitney in California.

If you were standing on top of that mountain, more than half of the atmosphere would be below you. At that height, the air pressure is half as strong as it is at the earth's surface. About half the amount of oxygen is left. This makes it hard to breathe.

Slowly, we continue to climb. Our instruments read 30,000 feet above sea level. Below us, a mountain pokes its top into the air. We are looking down at the highest mountain in the world, Mount Everest — about 29,000 feet high. The outdoor thermometer shows 55 degrees below zero — bitter cold!

Our balloon continues to climb — six, seven, eight, nine miles above the earth. We are still passing through the lowest part of the atmosphere, known as the troposphere. In Greek, *tropos* means to mix. In this layer of the atmosphere, the air is tumbled up and down with great fury, and winds blow fiercely in every direction.

As we leave the troposphere, the up-and-down bumpiness disappears. Strong winds — the jet streams — speed us smoothly along at more than 300 miles an hour. The outside thermometer reads 70 degrees below zero — which is a merciless cold.

By this time we are about twenty miles high, drifting upward through the next layer of air, the stratosphere. Here the air is clear, thin, and dry — no raindrops, no snowflakes, and almost no clouds.

We have reached a height of thirty miles, still rising through the stratosphere. The sun appears as a lone bright disk in a sky which is black, except for the many other stars shining through. There is very little dust to scatter the sun's rays, which brighten the daytime sky as seen from the earth.

The dust in Earth's atmosphere also blocks out the starlight traveling to Earth from far out in space. For stars are always shining, day and night.

Up here, the outside thermometer shows a sudden rise in temperature. The reading is 96 degrees, almost the same temperature as our bodies. Our chart tells us we must be passing through the ozone layer of the atmosphere.

Scientists have discovered that the ozone layer changes the powerful ultra-violet rays coming from the sun into harmless heat waves.

You might think of this ozone layer as a huge umbrella keeping most of these strong ultraviolet rays from reaching the earth. Although ultraviolet rays cannot be seen by the human eye, you know that some of them reach you — you become sunburned!

Our instruments tell us that we are fifty miles high. The temperature has dropped to 120 degrees below zero. A numb, cold, silent world surrounds us. We are in the top layers of the stratosphere.

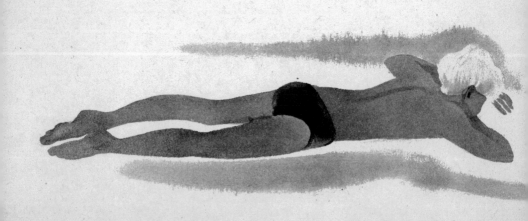

Above us, the atmosphere continues thinning out for hundreds of miles into outer space. Below us, the earth's surface is not clear. Cities, mountains, forests, and seas seem to be covered with a floating veil of darkened grays, greens, and browns.

It is now time for us to start our journey back to Earth. We open the helium valve. Slowly, the balloon begins to wrinkle; the helium gas is escaping. We stop rising. In a short time, we feel ourselves going down. We quickly close the valve, and keep descending slowly.

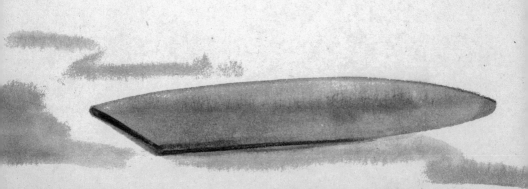

Once again, the troposphere greets us. No longer do we drift smoothly through the quietness of the stratosphere. Our cabin jerks from side to side. We are caught up in a game of tag between strong, gusting winds. Luckily, the game doesn't last long.

Below us, the earth rolls out into patches of browns and greens. Tall ponderosa pine trees guard the surrounding land.

In the distance, thin coils of gray smoke waft upward. Our balloon drifts closer. The smoke trails thicken and darken. The pine trees grow thin and small. Feeble branches have lost their needles. Many trees are dead. Bare earth shows through. For factory smokestacks have spread their unclean gases, poisoning the pine needles, which make the food needed by the growing tree.

Now we are no more than a thousand feet high. We begin to slow down . . . there is very little wind. Thick, heavy brown smoke hangs over the city. The floating haze seems to be anchored to the earth, with imprisoned smoke from coal fires and fumes from paint, steel, paper, and chemical factories.

Burning garbage dumps also send their wastes into this dirty air. Cars crawl like tiny bugs through a maze of city streets, leaving a trail of escaping gases which soon invade the atmosphere.

An atmosphere filled with smoke and gases from burning oil, gasoline, coal, and chemicals gives us sore throats, makes us cough, burns our eyes, and hurts our lungs.

Our atmosphere is precious. We must not use it as though it were a vacuum cleaner for the earth, sucking up the poisons we produce.

Nor must we use our oceans as a giant sink, to be a dumping ground for all the different wastes we do not use.

Both oceans — the ocean of water and the ocean of air — work together, keeping all the plants and animals alive upon our planet Earth.

All living things must have air and water . . . but if they are to survive, both the water and the air must be clean!

Index